BOHEMIAN
Daughters

Family Quest

ANTTONIA BARTEN

ISBN 978-1-7351812-0-2 (paperback)
ISBN 978-1-7351812-1-9 (hardcover)
ISBN 978-1-7351812-2-6 (digital)

Copyright © 2020 by Anttonia Barten

All rights reserved. No part of this publication may be reproduced, distributed, or transmitted in any form or by any means, including photocopying, recording, or other electronic or mechanical methods without the prior written permission of the publisher.

Printed in the United States of America

Prague Czech Republic, 1959–1968
Australia, 1968–1992

This book is dedicated to my grandmother and father. My wish is that this book will help those who have gone through traumatic times.

PREFACE

Legend has it that a beautiful Slovakian Princess stood on a hill overlooking the Vltava River at the place known as Vychirad. The Princess said, "A city known as Praha [Prague] will be built on this hill and surrounding area, and it will become famous". Prague was built in the ninth century, and its origin started from Vychirad and expanded. It is the historical capital of Bohemia.

The legend has come true, and after years of invasion and occupation by the Russians, Prague and the Czech Republic were part of the Eastern bloc. Today, it is prosperous, and tourists from all over the world visit Prague.

I was born in Prague, Czechoslovakia in 1959. In 1968, when Czechoslovakia was invaded and occupied by the Russians and placed under communist rule, I was nine years old. My mother and stepfather took me to Australia without telling my father.

Whilst growing up in an oppressive war environment would have been difficult, if I stayed in Prague, I would have been with people who loved me, and I would have been in my homeland, I had no choice. I was only 9 years old; I had no say whether to stay in Prague or to being taken away to Australia. I was an inconvenience and a hindrance to my mother, and she watched and allowed the stepfather to abuse me. Being in Australia, which is a free country, made no difference as I was oppressed at home and treated as a slave. I kept thinking of my father in Prague and how to find him.

One of my passions were books. I started reading books at the age of approximately five. I found I could dissociate myself from my environment, by getting engrossed in a book. My other passion was and remains travel.

Prague is a very cultural city with museums, theatres, and libraries. Some of them are very old and house rare books. In Prague is Strahov Monastery, near Prague Castle. Strahov Library is the second-oldest church library in Bohemia with uninterrupted existence. The library has around 280,000 titles, of which 3,000 are manuscripts, and 1,500 are incunabula. The oldest manuscript is the *Strahov Gospel*, dated 860.

Strahov Library.
I attribute this work to giggle the author and thank him/them/they for his/their contribution.

The Czech Republic is a small country in the centre of Eastern Europe. For a small country it has an abundance of natural beauty. It has mineral resources—including silver, gold, and plutonium—as well as mineral spas. There are forests, rivers, lakes, and mountains, as well as beautiful architecture, museums, theatres, and other treasures.

Germany invaded and occupied the Czech Republic before and after the Second World War. The Russian invasion and occupation began in August 1968 and lasted until approximately 1989. The Russians devastated Prague and stole many beautiful paintings, tapestries, gold, and many other treasures.

The Russians built horrible tower blocks, that were grey in color, and depressing, to house the Czech people. The Russian Communist regime, confiscated the Czech people's homes, land, and nice flats and units to either live in them, including the soldiers, or to sell them. The concrete towers, known as "the concrete jungle", the Czech people were forced to live in and had to pay rent to live in the concrete boxes.

Chapter 1

Russian Invasion and Occupation.

The Russian invasion and occupation began in August 1968. I was nine years old and on the last day of summer camp in Bohemia, Czechoslovakia. I was awakened at approximately 5:00 a.m. by a droning sound and a lot of wheels screeching. It was like many cars but much louder. I came out of my tent and looked up to see what looked like hundreds of planes overhead. I had no idea what was going on but felt very frightened. Other children and teachers came out of their tents and saw and pointed at the planes. The noise of the screeching wheels intensified.

Our teacher told us to go to the canteen and have something to eat. I could see the fear in her face. We then got our things packed, and the tents were taken down. A bus collected us to return to Prague. As we went through a small town, we could see many soldiers with machine guns; they wore green fatigues, and on their hats were red stars. Our teacher told us they were Russian. Also, the screeching was from many, many tanks. At the small square where we were stopped were many Russian soldiers, tanks, and trucks.

Three Russian soldiers boarded our bus. Our teacher told us to hide under the seats and not to come out. The Russian soldiers pointed the machine guns at our heads. Our teacher became upset and told them to stop, saying *"they are only children"*. They laughed. Suddenly, one of the soldiers grabbed our teacher by her hair and dragged her off the bus. The soldiers shot her point-blank in the head, and she fell slumped to the ground. We all witnessed it and were screaming and crying. The bus driver took off, with the doors still open, and headed for Prague as fast as he could. He was crying and shaking.

When we arrived in Prague, my grandmother met me at the bus stop. There was a lot of commotion. People were screaming, crying, and running around. The fear on their faces was terrible. The Russian soldiers were everywhere with their machine guns and many tanks and trucks. The tanks tore up tram tracks, all you could see was smoke and sparks coming from the wheels. They wounded people for absolutely no reason. Many people could not understand why this was happening, and shock and fear were on many faces.

The soldiers in tanks and those with machine guns, shot-up buildings, leaving a spray of bullet holes, or large holes made by the tanks. Again, why they did this, was mind-boggling?

My grandmother took me home immediately and told me not to say anything or look at the soldiers along the way. I could not understand what was happening. I told my grandmother about my teacher being shot, and she cried. Everyone was in shock, because it happened so quickly, and no one was told what was going on. Alexander Dubček held the seat of power at the time of the invasion. He lost his seat.

Downfall

On the night of 20–21 August 1968, Warsaw Pact forces except Romania entered Czechoslovakia. The occupying armies quickly seized control of Prague and the Central Committee's building, taking Dubček and other reformers into Soviet custody. But, before they were arrested, Dubček urged the people not to resist militarily, on the grounds that "presenting a military defense would have meant exposing the Czech and Slovak peoples to a senseless bloodbath." Later in the day, Dubček and the others were taken to Moscow on a Soviet military transport aircraft (reportedly one used in the invasion).https://en.wikipedia.org/wiki/Alexander_Dubček#Downfall. Text is available under the Creative Commons Attribution-ShareAlike License.

I attribute this text to the Wikipedia Commons and thank them for their contribution.

People in Prague surrounding Russian tanks and soldiers.
What you are seeing are Czech people surrounding the Russian tanks, confused and terrified.

Russian Invasion.
I attribute this work to Adam Jones, Ph.D. and thank him for his contribution to this historic photograph.

As will be seen from this photograph, on one side the 1968 Russian Invasion. The Czech people had terror on their faces and confusion. They did not carry any weapons, and to see so many tanks, trucks and Russian soldiers carrying machine guns and other weapons, it was confusing and senseless violence. On the other side the same area 50 years later peaceful.

After seeing our dear teacher shot, all the children including myself on the bus required intensive counseling and were given medication to help us cope.

During the invasion and occupation, there was a curfew. Beginning at 8:00 p.m., no one was allowed on the streets.

An old man I knew well was blind and deaf and lived in our neighborhood. He did not know about the curfew and had walked his little dog at the same time every night, just after eight, for many years. I was looking out of the window and saw some Russian soldiers at the end of our street. They did not call out or talk to the man. They just shot him.

I recall other terrible incidents whilst I was still in Prague. These have stayed with me all my life.

Chapter 2

Childhood in Prague (1959–1968)

My parents separated and divorced when I was approximately two years old. My mother was a party girl and didn't like any restrictions, such as having children.

My father came home one day to find my mother and a man who became my stepfather kissing. When the stepfather saw my father, he jumped out of a first-story window to avoid a confrontation or fight. Yet he abused children which will be explained later in the book.

After my parents divorced, my mother left me with anyone or anywhere, or on my own when I was as young as two years old.

When I was approximately three or four years old, I was left at an orphanage for months until my father found out and took me out.

I was left in a small cabin at night for hours; the only light was a fire. I was in a cot and could not get out.

I was also left in an empty apartment ten stories high. It was daylight, but when it started getting dark, I was very frightened.

I had no food, water, or milk, and it was cold. I climbed onto the central heating and to a window ledge. I sat there, crying and screaming. A neighbor saw me. She and her husband broke the door down and grabbed me before I fell. They gave me food and hot milk and put me to bed in their apartment. Then they called the police.

The police waited until my mother came to get me in the middle of the night. They took her to the police station and charged her with negligence and for endangering a child's life and abandonment.

After this incident, my grandmother took care of me. I was so happy because my grandmother loved me and took loving care of me. She was also extremely kind.

I felt a deep bond with my grandmother that I did not have with my mother. I have happy memories of my grandmother and how she took care of me, including taking me to a small cottage in the country. I remember catching a train and my uncle carrying me on his shoulders, to my grandmother's cottage. I remember being looked after by my grandmother, walking in the forest, and playing with the squirrels.

One time when I was sick and my mother left me on my own in the apartment, my grandmother walked a long way in the snow to bring me strawberries and take care of me.

I have many fond memories of my grandmother but very few of my mother.

There were only a couple of good memories that I have of my mother. One of those memories, that I remember. My mother took Emma and me to a lakeside village. It was summer and very hot. We stayed in a quaint guest house. My mother asked Emma and me to pick some cherries from the cherry tree on the property. Emma climbed the tree, whilst I stayed on the ground holding the basket. Suddenly, a branch broke, and Emma came flying down from the tree to the ground. When I saw this happening, I dropped the basket, and Emma landed in it. She looked so funny, like she was badly sunburnt, and peeling. She was covered in cherry juice and bits of cherries all over her. Unfortunately, she broke her arm and had it in a plaster cast, so for the rest of our stay, we could not swim. We would go into the nearby forest and pick wild blueberries and blackberries. The forest floor looked like it had a deep blue carpet.

I have also tried to remember my father. One of the only memories from my childhood, is when I was in winter camp, and he skied there to try to teach me how to ski. He was a champion cross-country skier. Unfortunately, I did not have the coordination or balance to ski, but I could ride and maneuver a sled.

I recall an incident at winter camp, and I was approximately 7 years old. A girl at the camp broke her leg, from the ankle up to her knee, whilst skiing, she was in a lot of pain. I did not know her, as she was not in my group of friends, but I was happy to help.

The camp was isolated, and we did not have a four-wheel drive, or tractor to get to the nearby village. The girl was in a lot of pain, and the teachers put her leg in a temporary splint. We had to get her to the nearby village for treatment, as soon as possible.

It was late in the afternoon, and it started to snow heavily. We tied 4 sleds together, and because I was fast and agile on a sled, I lead the other sleds. There were two teachers and the caretaker, a man approximately 30 years old, he took a rifle.

As we were making our way down a narrow track in the thick forest, we could hear wild animals rustling nearby, including wolfs howling, we were all very frightened, but the caretaker had the rifle ready, should we have been attacked. We got to the village just after dusk and took the girl to the doctor who put her leg in a plaster cast and gave her strong pain killers, and crutches.

We stayed the night in the village, and in the morning a tractor-pulled our sleds through the forest up to our camp.

Also, I recall my father stood on numerous occasions at my school fence and brought me gifts and ice cream. My mother would not allow my father to see me.

Apart from my terrible family life after my mother married my stepfather, I had a lot of friends and played with them often, and would not come home until it was late, to get away from my mother and stepfather. There were some very happy times, and after I was taken from Prague, I missed them. My friends sent a card with all their signatures to Australia. I also missed my grandmother and my other relatives.

I was not aware until I was in Australia how difficult and terrifying the invasion and occupation was for many Czech people. One student in Wenceslas Square burned himself alive in protest.

Whilst being in Australia saved me from the horror of the Russian invasion and occupation, I would have been better off in Prague with my grandmother or father, as the rest of my childhood in Australia was traumatic, abusive, and violent. This was caused by my stepfather. My mother watched the abuse but did nothing. I was also treated as a slave and had to do all the housework; I received no pocket money.

My mother married my stepfather shortly after she divorced my father. The stepfather was an evil, abusive man who regularly abused me on all levels. And at times, he abused his own daughters, Emma and Louise, both in Prague and after we got to Australia.

My mother severely punished Emma in Prague while accusing her of stealing some jewelry. She put Emma in an institution for a month. This was similar to when she put me in the orphanage.

My mother later found the jewelry, which she had misplaced.

Chapter 3

Kidnapped Prague Czechoslovakia (August 1968)

I was taken by my mother and stepfather from Prague to Australia. In August 1968, during the Russian invasion and occupation, my mother told my father she was taking me to Vienna to visit my aunty. She did not tell him she was taking me out of Czechoslovakia to Australia, which was on the other side of the world.

The journey started in the middle of the night. My mother woke me up and told me to get up because we were leaving. I was still half asleep and could not understand why she woke me. There was a lot of commotion, and my stepfather screamed at me. It appeared they were running away from something.

They took one suitcase for two adults and two children. I also had to leave behind my beloved teddy bear, which was small. I had that teddy bear since I was a baby, and I had it with me all the time. We were pushed into the car, and my stepfather drove away in a hurry.

The apartment was left as if we were still living there. I believe they were, in fact, running away from something other than the Russians. I believe my stepfather was Russian, and I was told that he spent time in a concentration camp. I said previously that he was evil. I also believe that he was mentally unstable.

My mother was a nursing sister, and my stepfather worked as a scientist in Prague. I recall going to his place of work. It was heavily guarded, including guard dogs. My mother also told me that she and my stepfather were working on some experiments with uranium and plutonium, both abundant in the Czech Republic, and experimenting with animals just before the invasion and occupation.

The drive from Prague to the Czech-Austrian border took approximately two hours. My mother and stepfather told Emma and me not to say anything when we got to the border.

I was crying and kept asking for my teddy bear. I was screamed at, so to pass the time, I watched the trees in the forest and pretended they were ghosts.

We arrived at 'checkpoint Charlie' on the Czech Republic and the Austrian border. There were many Russian soldiers with machine guns and bright lights that shone into the car. They asked my mother and stepfather a lot of questions, one of them being, "Where are you going and what's the reason?"

My stepfather, in Russian, replied, "To visit relatives in Vienna". They checked the passports and documents and looked around the car. They stared at Emma and me. They checked the boot and found one suitcase. They then waved us through.

We drove another two hours, and when we arrived at an old warehouse, it was still dark. The warehouse was a Red Cross hostel for Refugees. We knocked on the door, and a woman opened the door. My mother gave her some documents, and after reading them, she let us in. It was a huge warehouse, cold with what looked like thousands of beds very close together. We were shown to four beds. I found it very hard to sleep because there was a lot of noise and being very close next to strangers.

In the morning, we were given breakfast. I went outside to look around and see where Emma and I could play. The warehouse was surrounded by mounds of rubbish and dirt. We played where we could. It was terrifying with all the strange people—and so many of them, and we had to sleep near them.

We stayed at the Red Cross hostel for approximately four months. Then in December 1968, we were given airplane tickets and some documents to Australia. We were considered as political refugees.

Chapter 4

Austria to Australia, December 1968. Refugees.

We flew with Qantas. The plane trip was very long, and I became airsick. We arrived at Sydney airport in approximately the middle of December 1968. It was terribly hot, and I became sick. Australia seemed to me like an alien country, with people talking a strange language, and the heat and humidity were terrible. I didn't like Australia and kept thinking of Prague and my grandmother.

We were driven with the rest of the refugees in buses to a Detention Centre in Sydney. When we arrived, the buses were stopped at a high metal fence and high metal walls. What appeared to be guards came on board, stared at us, and checked our documents. It was so reminiscent of Prague; I became very frightened.

The driver was instructed to drive the bus in and stop at the intake building. My mother and stepfather went in. They could not understand what was being said to them as they did not speak English, but I think a translator may have helped them. They came out with a key with a number on it, and one of the guards took us to our very small cabin.

It was basically one room with a bed and bunks. There was no toilet or shower. We had to go outside for that.

To eat we had to go to a cafeteria. I remember strange food green jelly which was served often. To this day, I cannot eat green jelly.

I also encountered my first cockroach; there were no cockroaches in Czechoslovakia. I was in the shower block, and a big black cockroach came crawling out of the wooden slats on the floor. I screamed very loudly, and my mother came running and stepped on the cockroach.

There was not much to do at the detention centre. Emma and I played where we could, but the detention centre was like a prison to some extent, and we were not allowed outside of the detention centre.

Emma and I started our Australian schooling there. I was very keen to learn English fast, but Emma was reluctant. Adults also had English language classes. My mother attended, but my stepfather would not go.

I have not seen my mother or stepfather for many years, and they would be very old now. But when I last saw them, he still did not speak English well.

We had to remain at the detention centre for approximately six months.

Chapter 5

From Detention Centre to a New Life.

After six months, we were sent to a rented house in a quiet leafy suburb in Sydney. It was a nice, big, old house with a front yard and a decent size backyard in a good street.

My mother and stepfather worked in a factory so that they could pay the rent, bills, groceries, and so on. I remember the first shopping trip to buy groceries. My mother came back with a huge trolley full of groceries, meat, fruit, vegetables, and the like. I have never seen so much food in my life. Whilst Czechoslovakia is a beautiful country, it was a poor country. Food was terribly expensive, especially meat. Most of the time you had to buy what was available. Under the Communist regime, first-grade food went to the party members, and the Czech people were given second-grade food. They had to queue for it, sometimes for hours, in the freezing cold.

Emma and I started our education at the local primary school in Sydney. I found it strange at first but tried hard to assimilate. Emma struggled, especially with the language. She was very angry, especially if other children made fun of her; it was worse when boys ridiculed her. One time she picked up a boy and hurled him across desks. He hit the wall.

My mother found work at a large local hospital as a registered nursing sister. My stepfather still worked at the factory.

I mentioned my stepfather was evil, psychotic, and cruel. He liked native Australian animals and somehow got his hands on a wombat which he kept in the backyard. I named it Fatso. The wombat is a wild animal, and it died shortly after being taken out of its natural environment. I believe it is against the law to keep native Australian animals in captivity. I felt very sad about it. I remember my stepfather experimented with animals in Prague.

Emma and I made friends with a nice girl just down the street. Her father worked for Arnott's Biscuits, and under the house was a treasure trove of boxes of biscuits which we could eat. Emma and I went to our friend's home often to play, but she was not invited to our house because of my stepfather. Our friend had a Labrador dog, and he liked to steal shoes from the front of the houses and store them under the house, where the biscuits were. There was a mound of single shoes. He only stole one shoe, not the pair, and chewed them.

Approximately a year after we fled Czechoslovakia, my stepfather's oldest daughter, Louise, joined us at the rented house. She was able to leave Czechoslovakia without any problems, strengthening my belief that my mother and stepfather were running away from something—and it was not the Russians.

I believe they may have committed some crime against Czechoslovakia and fled to avoid legal action and/or prison.

Approximately two years after we moved to the rented house, we were offered a housing commission home in another suburb in Sydney, which my mother and stepfather took. It was a basic three-bedroom house with a huge backyard.

My stepfather acquired two goannas and snakes. The goannas were kept in a fenced enclosure in the backyard. He kept the snakes, pythons, in glass fish tanks. He often took the snakes out and played with them. He put them around Emma's neck, and she was terrified.

One day Emma and I got home from school to find a lot of neighbors at the front of our house and at the back. They told us the goannas had gotten out and were in a pine tree at the back of our house. As they pointed at them, Emma and I, armed with hessian bags and sticks, climbed the tree and caught the goannas. It was very dangerous as they have very sharp claws and strong tails. And they bite. Plus, we had to balance on the branches of the tree. The enclosure where they were kept was made of chicken wire and had no concrete foundation, so the goannas dug themselves free.

We did not get a thank you from my stepfather. The entire neighborhood disliked the stepfather and called him weird. They felt sorry for us.

One night an intruder tried to climb into my mother and stepfather's window. We had an Alsatian dog my stepfather kept in the bedroom. I think he knew the people and kids in our neighborhood disliked him, so he kept it for protection. The intruder did not try and break in to steal, but I believe to harm my stepfather. The Alsatian jumped out the window and chased the intruder.

I mentioned previously my stepfather liked to keep Australian native animals. He also liked to keep animals that bite, including a ferret. He put the ferret on Emma's shoulder. She was terrified and would not move. The ferret did not bite her, but it was another bizarre act of my stepfather's.

He also asked Louise to get him a crocodile; she did. He kept it in the bathtub. One night I was going to have a bath. I did not turn on the light and had no idea the crocodile was there. When I put my feet in the bath, it bit me. Like the wombat, the crocodile died a short time after my stepfather got it.

The walls of the house were covered in wood paneling (very seventies). My stepfather's other bizarre hobby was collecting hideous masks from New Guinea. If you walked into the lounge room in the dark, the masks stood out, and they were frightening. He also kept a fully loaded rifle in the house. He was paranoid and thought people were out to get him.

When my mother and stepfather went away, I invited my friends over. They found the place frightening and weird because of the masks. They also made comments that it felt uncomfortable. They did not stay long and never came back. I did not invite my friends over again but went to their homes instead.

I mentioned previously that the people and children in our neighborhood did not like my stepfather, and I don't think they liked my mother either. One night there was a bright light near the fence; the bright light was a fire. Someone lit the dry bamboo cane (dry) which covered the fence and set it alight. The fence burned down, and my stepfather had to put up a new one.

My stepfather was offered a position with an Australian Science Company. No one would work with him because they disliked him. So, he was moved into the basement on his own. I don't know what he did, but I hope it was not experimenting on animals.

Chapter 6

Thirteen to Eighteen Years Old - Truth.

When I turned thirteen, my mother finally told me the truth, after years of lying. She never wanted me and that I was a mistake because there was no "pill" at that time. She also told me my father was evil and sadistic and wanted to "chop my head off with an axe". She claimed my stepfather was a good man, but I did not believe her. That was devastating enough, but then Emma told me my stepfather was not my father. I already knew that, but my mother tried very hard to convince me, since I was little, that he, in fact, was my father. It became obvious that my mother is an accomplished liar and manipulator. I had a clear understanding and purpose of what I needed to accomplish, and that was finding my father, although at that time I had no idea how or when? I felt free in my mind and felt like a heavyweight was lifted off my shoulders. I thought hard how to find my father and decided that I would start by writing to him. Even though I still had to endure abuse from the stepfather and to some point from my mother, I could escape the pain, by planning and thinking of what it would feel like to find and meet my father.

I sat at my window at night and prayed, on how to find my father.

I asked my mother for my father's address. She was hesitant but eventually gave me an address, and I started writing letters in English. Even though I did not receive a response, I kept writing in the hope that my father received them. I ask myself this question to this day. If my mother did not love me, and I was an inconvenience and a hindrance, why did she take me from Prague? I believe one of the reasons was to hurt my father.

When we emigrated to Australia, my mother changed my name to my stepfather's surname. I had no choice in the matter, but I am still angry about it and dislike that surname. I felt as though she took away my identity.

After primary school, I attended a Sydney high school. I loved school because it was an escape from the terrible abuse at home. In high school, I achieved a Higher School Certificate. I spent most of my time in the library after school so that I did not have to go home, and I enjoyed reading and doing research. At one time, I felt so depressed that I took an overdose of sleeping pills and went to school. I collapsed in class and was taken to the sickbay. The nurse rang the ambulance, and I had to have my stomach pumped at the hospital. My mother was called but did not turn up for hours.

It was suggested that I see a psychiatrist, and my mother took me to one. He spoke to both of us and then to me on my own. His conclusion was that there was nothing mentally wrong with me. But there was something wrong with my parents, and my home life was a nightmare which had a terrible effect on me.

I was approximately 14 years old and had to basically fend for myself, including buying my own textbooks, stationery, and so on for school. As I mentioned before, even though I did all the housework, I did not receive any pocket money. I found a job at Grace Brothers, in a nearby suburb. I started to work for two perfume companies, Leon Worth and Madam Rocha. Both were very strong perfumes. And when men wanted to know how they smelled, I had to test them on myself. On the bus trip back home, no one wanted to sit near me as I smelled so much of the two perfumes.

I continued to work at Grace Brothers until I was about sixteen as well as going to school.

Because I commenced work at an early age, I was able to travel at the age of eighteen to Tahiti. It was fantastic, and as I mentioned earlier, travel, as well as reading, has always been a passion.

Also, when I was approximately sixteen years old, my grandmother made the very long trip from Prague to Australia (approximately twenty-three hours one way) to see my mother and me. She was always very petite but a very strong person. When I saw her, she looked very frail. When we had dinner, she left half the meal on the plate and tried to hide it under the table. No matter how often we told her it was all right, there was plenty of food here, she would still do it. I remember the food was sometimes scarce in Prague when I was a child. And what was available were vegetables but very little meat, or it was very expensive, so you made do with what was available.

My grandmother and I spoke alone, and what I could understand (she did not speak English) was that she had very high regard for my father, saw him regularly, and they spoke about me. But she disliked my stepfather. I begged her to take me back with her to Prague, but she could not. I gave her a letter written to my father. She promised to give it to him. She was aware of the abuse I received from my mother and stepfather but could do nothing. I believe she spoke to my mother about it. I have always loved my grandmother and have never stopped loving her, and I am grateful that she took care of me when I was a child.

Unfortunately, when my grandmother returned to Prague, she passed away. I did not find out straightaway. No surprise as my mother was always secretive and deceitful.

I wanted to move out of the home when I was eighteen because I could not stand my stepfather or mother. But my stepfather begged me to stay because he and my mother had a son. My mother preferred to work than looking after her son. My mother would not win the "Mother of the Year" award. I had to care for him full time. As my mother left me wherever and with whomever when I was small, she packed her son off to live overseas with relatives for a year because she found it difficult to cope with him when he got older.

At high school, I excelled in history, English, and home economics (cooking). I came top in the state in home economics. I met a man whilst on holiday in the south of Sydney and wanted to run away with him. My home economics teacher came to my home and spoke with my mother and me, saying I should not waste my life on this man. I should think of my future and continue to study home economics. I took her advice and stayed. I saw the man years later. He was bald and had no teeth. I was glad that I took my home economics teacher's advice.

After completing year 12 (high school certificate), I was not sure what I wanted to do. I know I could have done much better, except in year 5 (today it's year 11 in Australia), I met a girl with very similar traits and personality as myself, and we became best friends. For this book, I will call her Carol. Carol and I became inseparable, and we lived very close to each other. Carol brought some weed (marijuana) to school one day, and she smoked it in the girls' toilets. It was old and stale, and she was "off her head". The toilet had two entrances. Two PE teachers, the two worst female teachers at school, came in. One came from one entrance, and the other came from the other. We were cornered. Carol was dancing with a mop.

I saw both teachers approaching and tried to warn Carol, but she could not hear me. Carol was not caught smoking the weed, but both teachers could smell it. Carol and I were given detention for a month. I did not mind because I was with Carol and did not have to go home.

In year 12, we had what was called "muck-up day" (it's no longer held). It is the best day of the entire twelve years of high school. It's like fun graduation, and the school leavers are given the full run of the school. You can do what you like! You come to school dressed in old clothes because, during the day, shaving foam, eggs, flour, water bombs, rotten tomatoes, oranges, and other things are thrown at you. Also, you are allowed—within reason—to throw things at the teachers you dislike. One of the PE teachers was at school that day, but the other was not.

The day started early, at six in the morning, and we (the school leavers) dressed the school. For example, we put toilet paper over doors and windows, and Vaseline and shaving cream on the toilet seats. We set up the stocks, where people get locked in. Water, flour bombs, and rotten fruit are thrown at them, as well as eggs. They are covered in shaving foam and feathers. We also brought magnums of champagne to drink and spray people with. The other kids loved it because it was entertaining.

The high school had a concrete platform outside the windows on the top floors, so we set up chairs there. The platform overlooked the quadrangle and assembly area. We waited until nine o'clock when the assembly was held; you were not allowed to throw anything until the assembly was over. I saw the PE teacher, and straight after assembly, I threw a rotten tomato at her and got her in the face. She looked around to see who threw it at her. She could not see me because the sun was in her eyes. I got her back for years of what she did to me, including detention for no reason (apart from the incident with Carol and smoking pot). Another reason this PE teacher disliked me was that she also dealt with Emma. And since Emma was no angel, she thought I was the same as Emma.

Carol was in year 5. She dressed in old clothes instead of a uniform. They were not allowed to get involved in muck up day. Carol grabbed me and put me in the stocks and locked it. Then she rubbed eggs, flour, and shaving cream in my hair. After that, she let me go. I threw a flour and water bomb at her. Carol continued the rest of the day, as a Year 6 student. We had so much fun. By the end of the day, year 6 students and the school were covered in flour, eggs, toilet paper, and rotten fruit. We had to go home and get cleaned up because that night was our formal night or prom night. I had a very difficult time getting all the muck out of my hair; it took about five washes.

The formal night was excellent. The school hired bands well known in Australia, Sherbet with Daryl Braithwaite and Dragon with Mark Hunter.

I stayed in contact with Carol after I left school. I believe she may have gone to university after she completed year 12.

CHAPTER 7

Eighteen to Twenty-Eight Years Old – Freedom.

Leaving the oppressive violent and abusive home life, at approximately 21 years old,, was freedom. My first apartment was a "granny flat", whilst it was small, it was very comfortable.

I could have done much better in my higher school certificate, but I chose to party with Carol instead. I asked for a transfer from Grace Brothers at a nearby suburb to one of its stores closer to where I lived. Approximately after a year of working there, Grace Brothers sold the store to Myers, another department store chain. I worked my way up to assistant manager in the Miss Boutique, a fashion department for teenagers and young people. I wanted to work in the city and applied to Grace Brothers in Sydney. I was successful and again worked in fashion. This was in approximately 1978.

I worked at Grace Brother in the city for approximately six months. I came to work every day, but this day was going to be different. I don't exactly recall when this happened, but it was approximately 1978. There were sirens, mainly in Pitt Street in Sydney City. The Hilton Hotel and Grace Brothers were opposite each other in Pitt Street.

People were running, screaming, and yelling, and the police with loudspeakers telling them to get out of the area. Suddenly, the sirens intensified, and it was then I and other staff members went to the window to have a look. Almost the entire area of Pitt Street surrounding the Hilton Hotel was cleared except for parked cars, police cars, fire trucks, and the special bomb unit. A man came out of the bomb unit vehicle dressed in very thick protective gear from head to toe and set up the robot.

There was a bomb in one of the rubbish bins outside the Hilton Hotel. The robot came slowly to the rubbish bin and pulled out the bomb, which from memory was wrapped in something, like a cloth. It was at this stage that our supervisor told us to move away from the window and to hide under tables, behind counters, and so on. We did as she instructed.

A few minutes later, there was an ear-piercing explosion as the robot detonated the bomb. The windows at Grace Brothers exploded. Glass shattered and rained onto the floor. At the same time, very heavy steel shutters came down on the windows and doors. There was very heavy smoke and a terrible smell. The entire floor I was on was covered in smoke and a terrible smell. I heard windows in surrounding buildings in Pitt Street explode and the glass shattering onto the pavement.

After the explosion, there was an eerie silence and still a lot of smoke. We were instructed to go home so that repairs and replacement of glass could be carried out and the choking smoke, that seemed to hang around forever, cleared. If people were not evacuated and the bomb detonated, the casualties would have been horrific.

I loved the job, but after a couple of years, I wanted a change to a more career-oriented position. I started a receptionist/secretarial course at college. It took approximately six months to complete. I also studied other courses, including computer programming, workplace assessment, and training, and completed an IT Diploma. Now, I am studying for a Diploma in Events Management. I have always enjoyed studying and reading. Knowledge is power!!

My first job after finishing my course was with a firm of architects in North Sydney. Some of my duties included reception, secretarial, ammonia printing, and going on-site with the architects and taking notes. I left that position for a better one in specialized insurance. The company insured livestock but primarily thoroughbred horses and racehorses. We insured a famous racehorse. I really enjoyed this job because of my love for animals, and I was a keen horse rider.

The insurance company was bought out by a larger insurance company, and I worked for the finance manager with the new insurance company. I had the best boss. We played squash in the mornings before work, and I attended client luncheons.

Whilst I had a great job and good friends, I wanted to travel to London. In the back of my mind, I was hoping to somehow find my father, but I had no idea how. I thought about this for a while, and when I decided I wanted to go. I had a garage sale and sold everything I had. I bought a four-liter backpack and a one-way ticket to London via Los Angeles. I gave two weeks' notice at work and left just two weeks after I made the decision and I had no plans when to return to Australia.

Chapter 8

1987 - Travel from Australia to London. Adventure. "Winging It".

I had no idea where I was going to stay or work, so I winged it. As I boarded the plane, I felt a calmness, no anxiety or stress. On the flight to Los Angeles, I met two girls and their mother, who were also traveling to London via Los Angeles. We talked most of the way to Los Angeles, and the mother suggested I stay with them. I took her up on the offer.

When we got to Los Angeles, it was hot. The hotel we stayed in had a pool which was a relief, and we used it extensively. I was interested in going to Disneyland. The girls and their mum thought it was a good idea, so we all went together. Disneyland is huge, and one day is not enough, so we bought a three-day pass. It was lots of fun, and we managed to fill the three days.

I only wanted to stay in Los Angeles for a week. The girls and their mum had also only booked their stay for a week.

I found Los Angeles rather boring. I was amazed at the size of some of the people who ate at McDonald's. The burgers and meals were twice as big as in Australia.

It was interesting nevertheless, and I always like experiencing new cultures and meeting new people.

I suggested we take a trip to Mexico, which was not far from Los Angeles, so we went to Acapulco, by bus. It was even hotter, but we were determined to find the real culture and people rather than just "where the tourists go". We found a quaint market and a taverna nearby. I bought a bright woven blanket (which I have to this day). We went to the taverna for a drink. It was lovely and cool. The barman brought over a tequila bottle with the worm on the bottom. I was game to try it, but my friends were not. This was a good thing because the worm acts like LSD, and I was "off my face". My friends helped me back on the bus. I believe I slept all the way back to Los Angeles.

I boarded the plane to London, as did my friends. Again, the trip took no time at all because my friends and I had so much to discuss.

When we landed in London, I had nowhere to stay, and again my friends suggested I stay with them. I was happy about that as I had never been to London and was a bit anxious and we all got on so well. London is an amazing place, but crowded, full of people and the pace was fast and everyone seemed to rush.

I stayed with my friends at their relatives' home but felt that I was intruding. So, I moved to a boarding house and stayed there for a few months while looking for a small flat. Accommodation in London is very hard to find and extremely expensive.

I had no trouble finding work. I worked in many companies and firms as a temporary, although some of my contracts went to long term. Among the businesses I worked for were;

- Engineers
- Banks
- Solicitors
- Publishers
- Advertising/Marketing
- London Council.

Whilst working, I planned my travel. I stayed friends with the girls and their mother, and the girls and I decided to travel to Scotland, the Shetland Islands, and other places in England. We caught the ferry to the Shetland Islands. On the ferry, we met a couple of Norwegian divers. I became friends with one of them, and he invited me to Oslo. I told him I would take him up on his offer and contact him when I was getting close to travelling to Norway.

We ended up in a pub on the Shetland Islands. It was full of Norwegians, including the two divers. I danced the whole night with the one I had made friends with on the way over. At that time of the year, there was light twenty-four hours all week in the Shetland Islands, making it hard to tell time. It was early morning, and my girlfriends and I booked accommodation and went to bed.

The Shetland Islands are quite desolate, and there is not much to do. In our travels, we came across some Shetland ponies. The Shetland ponies are amazing. I put my sunglasses on one and took his picture. He posed for the photo.

The Shetland Islands are a desolate, windy, and cold place. We noticed a large ship anchored offshore and asked why it was there. We were told it was a Russian prisoner ship. Instead of being in prison on land, they serve their time on the ship.

After the Shetland Islands, we caught the ferry back to the mainland and then a train to Scotland. The scenery was beautiful. We travelled around many parts of Scotland. The only place we missed seeing was Loch Ness (which I want to see someday). Scotland is a hauntingly beautiful place, but even in summer, it is windy and cold.

We stayed in quaint pubs. We booked a tour of a haunted castle and stayed the night. It was an experience, and whilst we heard strange noises, it was not like something out of a movie and not that frightening.

Chapter 9

Adventure – Travel on My Own: Europe.

The girls went back to London, and I was booked on a Contiki tour from Edinburgh to travel around Europe. I was in a pub, waiting for the bus, and started talking to an elderly couple from Edinburgh. I could barely understand what they were saying, but we communicated well enough to understand each other. I remember talking about Australia, and they told me they lived all their lives in Edinburgh but would like to travel one day to Australia and other countries.

They kept buying me drinks, and I became quite drunk. When I looked at the time, I had missed the bus. I telephoned Contiki, and they advised me another bus would run from Edinburgh tomorrow morning. The couple were kind enough to put me up for the night, and I felt like an adopted daughter. I had a nice hot bath and a warm meal. They tucked me into bed and promised to wake me early enough to catch my bus. I thought about what lovely people they were, but somewhat lonely.

I caught the bus, and the first stop was London to pick up more passengers; the bus was full. I remember hearing different accents. Our first stop was Paris, where we stayed for three nights. What I had heard of Paris was that it was a wonderful place, and I fell in love with it. French was one of the subjects at school I passed, but I was a bit rusty. Paris is a stunning city, full of history, charm, and architecture. I have always been interested in historical architecture. We had enough time to do the sightseeing at our own pace and going where we wanted to go. I found when I started travelling it is better to go where the tourists don't go (sort of don't follow the sheep) as you get to know the culture and people of that country much better. And you have more fun.

Our hotel was right in the old district. The old district had a lot of quaint cobbled streets with artists painting on the footpaths. I bought a painting of Paris. I remember trying my first frog legs and snails, both delicious. The only thing I could not stomach was steak tartare, which basically is raw mince.

What struck me as a complete opposite is that though Paris was renowned for its fashion and perfumes, the public toilets are basically a hole in the ground with a toilet seat. I found that disgusting.

The Eiffel Tower was amazing and the view spectacular. I did not feel comfortable, however, as I have had a fear of heights from my childhood [perched on a window ledge on the tenth floor].

The next country on the itinerary was Germany. I was not too taken with Germany. I remember travelling on the highway in Germany, and it was amazing as the traffic went at great speed.

We stopped in Munich for the day. In Munich, we stopped at the car museum and had a quick look around. The next stop was Bavaria. I enjoyed Bavaria, and the food and architecture were amazing. I bought a small stein as a souvenir. We stayed the night in a quaint traditional Bavarian hotel.

Early in the morning we boarded the bus and made our way to Switzerland. Switzerland is such a pretty place and very clean. We arrived at Lucerne around lunchtime. We ate in an outdoor café that served traditional Swiss food; a cheese fondue followed by a rich chocolate cake. Switzerland borders France, Germany, and Italy, so many of the foods are derived from those cultures.

Lucerne is a beautiful place built around a large lake. It is also surrounded by steep hills and mountains. The hotel we stayed in was on top of a mountain, and you got to it by cable car. On steep hills, I saw cows with bells around their necks. The sound was almost like music.

When we reached our hotel, it was shrouded in fog and quite cold. But the view of not only Lucerne but other towns and villages was spectacular. The hotel was very comfortable and had a big fire. You could sit around and drink hot chocolate with marshmallows.

At this point in the tour, I had two men interested in me. One was a redhead from New York, and the other a big man from Canada. The New Yorker proposed to me at the hotel we were staying in. I had to tell him no but was very flattered by his proposal.

It was time to leave, and I did not want to leave Lucerne. It is another place I will go back and see. The bus headed to Italy.

The view was amazing at every turn, and we were very lucky with good weather.

The beauty of Europe is that it is compact. Unlike Australia, where you must travel days to get to a city such as Melbourne, in Europe it is only a matter of hours.

We arrived in Rome in the afternoon. The tour guide told us the hotel name and said our bags would be in our rooms. We were free to explore Rome but had to be back at the hotel for dinner. We teamed up in groups, and my two admirers were in my group.

I heard that the Italians were amorous and passionate, but I had no idea they pinched backsides. By the end of the afternoon, my backside was sore and bruised.

Our group stopped around the Trevi Fountain for some lunch and coffee. It was a hot day, and we sat around the fountain and threw in money and made a wish. The big Canadian picked me up and threw me into the fountain. Other people jumped in, and we had a water fight. I noticed security, or the police, and called out to the others in the fountain to get out, which they did. The security officer did not say anything but hung around to make sure we did not do that again.

I have always been a coffee lover, but the coffee in Italy was divine.

The group then walked to the colosseum. It was interesting for the historical value but completely overrun with cats. And it smelled terrible. We decided to make our way to the hotel.

The next day there were some organized tours of Rome. After lunch, the bus headed to Florence. Florence is a beautiful city, full of culture. I much preferred Florence to Rome. There were some organized sightseeing tours the first day; the second day, we were free to explore Florence on our own. The hotel we stayed in was a small boutique hotel with a lot of character. It was in the city, so everything I wanted to see was close by. I headed to the Uffizi Museum, which has incredible paintings and statues, I enjoy museums, galleries, opera, ballet, and theatre. The statue of David was amazing, and the detail involved, it must have taken a long time. I wandered around and saw more sights and did some shopping, especially leather goods, and then headed for the hotel.

In the morning, after breakfast, the bus headed to Venice. What an amazing city built on water. The architecture and ambiance were out of this world. We were only in Venice for a short time but got some sightseeing in and a ride in a gondola with my two admirers. I loved Venice and will return.

After lunch, the bus headed for Amsterdam. I was not sure what to expect. On the bus, I got a bad cramp in my foot, and the big Canadian said, "I can fix that". He bent my toes so far back that he broke them. I arrived in Amsterdam with a plaster cast on my foot. Our hotel was in the red-light district, and prostitutes were displayed in windows.

Whilst the others explored Amsterdam, I sat in the hotel bar with my foot propped up, watching the prostitutes and other people in the street. It was interesting and passed the time. I did attend the group photograph, and we all dressed up in Dutch costume and clogs. I did not wear my clogs but bought a pair for when I could put them on my feet.

CHAPTER 10

Back in London: Accommodation, Work. Holiday - Oslo Norway.

The bus then headed for London. I did not know where I was going to stay, but the travel insurance covered accommodation and living expenses whilst I recuperated. After the cast came off, I had some rehabilitation and then went back to work.

I decided to travel to Norway and contacted my friend. He invited me to Oslo. He picked me up from the airport, and I stayed in the spare room in his apartment; he was a complete gentleman. Whilst he was at work, I cleaned the apartment and went shopping at the local supermarket to get groceries for dinner. Whilst the language was difficult to understand, I pretty much found what I wanted. I am not a bad cook, and my friend enjoyed the dinner I prepared for him.

On the weekend, my friend and his other friends decided to go diving in the fiords. They had a caravan we stayed in whilst they were diving. The landscape is very barren and freezing. The water in the fiords must be well below zero. I watched them put on their wetsuits. They first covered themselves in a solid fat paste which acted as an insulator. The wetsuits were made of three insulated layers and covered them from head to toe. All you could see were their eyes.

They were diving for hours. When they came out, they wanted hot coffee. They pulled out a bottle containing a clear liquid; it was rocket fuel. You can only drink it in coffee, but it really warms you up. Alcohol was prohibited in Norway at that time. The only alcohol you could buy in bars or restaurants was Bacardi Rum.

I tried some of the rocket fuel, and it went straight to my head.

My friend showed me around Oslo. We went dancing at a nightclub. We had a great time.

I have always been interested in reindeers and nature. I booked a tour through the forest. You sit in a sled with fur and blankets wrapped around you. The sled is pulled by four reindeer, and they are beautiful creatures. The trip through the forest was amazing. Everything was covered in snow, and it looked like a fairy tale.

I stayed for a week with my friend and then had to return to London. I thanked him very much for a wonderful time and for being a good host. I have not seen him since, although I do think of him occasionally.

I had to move out of the accommodation and found an old house in the CBD of London and shared it with other travellers. The house was in such a bad state that if you sat at the kitchen table and looked straight up, you could see the floor of the bathroom. The big bulge was the bathtub. We took bets who would land on the kitchen table in the bathtub. The accommodation was warm, and it was okay. I landed an amazing job working for a French Baron and Baroness who resided very close by.

I began working for the Baron as his assistant and secretary. The only problem was he had no idea how to use a computer and managed to break them. Every morning was the same; the computers were down, and it took hours for the IT person to fix them.

The Baroness asked me if I wanted to work for her, and I said yes. I was the Baroness's personal assistant and enjoyed the job very much. I accompanied her while shopping, on outings, and meetings.

When the Baron and Baroness's daughter was getting married, the Baroness asked me to arrange the wedding. I was terrified in case I stuffed up. But I set to work preparing, arranging, and planning the wedding. It was a massive job, from some five hundred wedding invitations to flowers (all white or cream); the bride's dress was organized by the designer. The cake had five layers and was a cream color with cream roses. There was much more organizing and planning. The reception was held in a castle. The Baroness bought me an exquisite gown for the wedding, as well as other beautiful clothes.

As I said, I was terrified. But apparently, I did an amazing job. It is easy when you have an unlimited budget. I kept notes of everything and followed through in detail. The preparation for the wedding went smoothly. I have since graduated in Diploma of Event Management. Whilst, I don't want to get into wedding management. I would love to manage Events in my home town of Prague, Czech Republic.

I wanted to stay with the Baron and Baroness, because they were very kind, caring and down to earth people, they made me feel like I was part of the family. They told me that my work was excellent. The only thing missing was I did not speak, write, or read fluent French, so I had to leave. If I did speak fluent French, I probably would have remained with them.

CHAPTER 11

Receiving News about My Father. Getting Married

After I stopped working with the Baron and Baroness, I started contract work with the Lloyds Bank in London as a data entry operator. My shifts were at night, and I worked with a group of nice girls. Whilst we were all hard workers, we also had lots of fun.

One night as I tried to input as much data before knockoff time, I received a telephone call on my mobile. It was a man, and guessing from his voice, he was mature. And he spoke with an unusual accent. He told me words to the effect, "Can you please come and see me? I have news about your father". I first thought it might be a setup, but the man knew a lot about my father. And how did he know my phone number? Then I thought, *He is my father!* I told him I would come, and he gave me the address in London and the day and time to come and see him.

The girls I worked with were curious about the telephone call. I explained how I was taken out of Prague by my mother and stepfather when I was approximately nine years old when the Russians invaded and occupied Czechoslovakia, and my father was not told they were taking me to Australia. I shared that I was only two years old when my mother and father divorced, so I didn't know him but was desperate to meet him. The story had the girls in tears.

I turned up at the address with a friend, just in case, it was a setup or something dangerous. From memory, he was a very pleasant-looking man in his sixties and wore a cardigan. I could also hear a female voice. I really thought at that stage he was my father, so I threw my arms around him. He showed me inside and told me he was not my father but a very close friend of his. I sat down. His wife, a very nice person, explained they were from Prague but were now living in London. The man told me he and my father had been friends for many years and still corresponded.

I asked him questions about my father, and he was happy to answer them. I explained to him that my mother told me very little about my childhood in Prague, relatives, and my father.

He told me my father received all my letters and how sad he felt about what I had to go through (abuse) at the hands of my stepfather and mother. He shared that my father missed me and was really looking forward to meeting me.

The man told me it would not be long before the Russians were ousted from Czechoslovakia and that my father really wanted to meet me. He also explained that because of the communist regime in Czechoslovakia, everything that came in and went out—letters, parcels—were opened and scrutinized. That was why my father could not write back to me. But there was another reason. My father was part of the resistance, and to write to me would have been extremely dangerous for him and, (as I was about to find out when I met him), for his wife and children.

I left feeling like I just won the lotto. After so many years of wondering if he loved me, got my letters, and if he wanted to see me, I had a lot of emotions and a lot of questions. But I was also very excited and found it hard to sleep that night.

I met this man a couple of more times. He showed me and translated a letter from my father to me. Part of the letter read, "I am so looking forward to seeing you, and it won't be too long before you can come home". After meeting this man and hearing about my father, I made inquiries about entering Czechoslovakia and was told it was too dangerous, and the Communist Regime wanted a lot of moncy from me to enter my homeland.

Around this time, I met a man named Bruce, who was to become my husband. Bruce also had wonderful friends, and I became very close to one couple. The woman, I will call her Suzan, and I became very close and spent a lot of time together.

My best friend from Australia, Carol, came to London. I was thrilled. Carol and Suzan were my bridesmaids when I got married in 1989. Carol met her husband in London and got married. It was one of her dreams to get married and have children. I am not sure where she is now, but I would love to see her again.

Bruce and I did the right thing and invited my mother to our wedding. It was the worst decision we made. My mother was ungrateful even though we paid for her airfare. She kept comparing her two weddings and that she did not have what I have. My stepfather called continually, and at one stage, he told my mother he fell off a ladder and hurt himself and that she had to come home. I was not sad to see her leave, especially since she gave us no consideration or was grateful for what Bruce and I did for her. Apparently, when she got back to Australia, my stepfather gave her a big bunch of roses. He never gave my mother flowers before.

CHAPTER 12

The "Velvet Revolution" in Prague. Finding and Meeting My Father.

Vaclav Havel started the Velvet Revolution (17 November 1989 to 29 December 1989) to drive the communist regime (Russians) out of Czechoslovakia. He was to become the first President of the Czech Republic [renamed from Czechoslovakia].

The Velvet Revolution began with a peaceful, non-violent protest against the communist regime. At the same time, what was known as Czechoslovakia became two new nations, the Czech Republic and the Slovak Republic. There were still some Russian soldiers hiding in farms, and refusing to leave after the regime was thrown out of the Czech Republic.

Velvet Revolution.
I attribute this work to ŠJů and thank him very much for his contribution to this important and historic photograph.

I heard from my father's friend around November 1989 that the Velvet Revolution to oust the Russians from Czechoslovakia had begun, and my father would contact him once Prague is safe. After Christmas 1989, my father contacted his friend and told him the regime had been overthrown, and the Russians had left the Czech Republic. When I was advised of this, I booked a flight in early January 1990 to Prague.

I flew from London to Prague. It was winter, and Prague was cold. But I didn't mind the cold; I was too excited to feel it. When I emerged from customs, a mix of emotions was swirling in my head and I had no idea what my father looked like, but he knew me straight away and came over. The feeling of joy, happiness, elation, and a feeling of being on cloud nine flooded me. I also felt, like "I am home". As we hugged each other, I started to cry.

Unfortunately, my father did not speak English. I met my stepmother, half-sister, half-brother, and half-sister's boyfriend, who could speak fluent English, so that made it a bit easier. I talked constantly and asked questions. I was told politely to be quiet, and that I could talk as much as I liked when we got to the unit.

I looked out the window as we drove from the airport, trying to remember when I was nine (I was now approximately twenty-nine), and to what Prague looked like then and now. Prague looked like it had been through a war zone. The buildings were shabby, and some had bullet holes, and unkept, the roads had potholes, and the streets were dirty.

My father drove a Skoda, communist issue. It was basically a box on wheels, but it ran well.

We arrived at the units where my father and his family lived. I could immediately tell the communists build them. They were grey ugly towers with a park around them. When you entered, it was as depressing inside as it was outside. They were referred to as "concrete jungle" My parents' unit was quite spacious and very clean. My father had the entire family working on the unit, painting, and cleaning before I arrived. I said, "I am not the queen. It is not necessary to go to all the trouble".

My father and I were smokers. My stepmother told us to either smoke outside, which was cold or stand under the exhaust fan in the kitchen.

The language barrier was a bit of a problem, but we used a bit of initiative and improvisation. For example, when talking about chickens, I flapped my arms. That had my family in tears from laughing. The strangest thing is, I was only nine years old when I was taken away, so I had primary school language education, and had spoken in Australia English, but bits of the Czech language started coming back. I found I could understand my father much better as time went on, and he could understand me. This was a relief as we spent a lot of time together, talking and going to various places, enjoying each other's company and having a lot of fun. I felt very comfortable in his company and found we started to bond and our relationship grew stronger and stronger. My father was also a bit of a comedian and made me laugh often.

The first night we sat under that exhaust fan, talking and talking and smoking, until the early hours. I had so many questions to ask him. One came up about my mother and stepfather. I could see my father was very angry and sad. He started to cry. He admitted he knew what was going on in Australia, me being abused, but he could do nothing about it. He also explained he never knew my mother planned to take me to Australia. All he was told was that we were going to see an aunt in Vienna. I told him I understood that he could do nothing to help, but I would have been far happier living with him, even though Prague was occupied by the Russians. My father said that if my mother entered Prague there will be trouble. He was very angry, and so was I because of what happened and the type of person she is and hurt a lot of people. By taking me away, I missed a lot of years being with my father, until now. I did not ask him any more questions as I did not want to upset him further. I did, however, raise the matter of my mother telling me that he tried to cut off my head with an axe. We both laughed at how absurd and twisted that was. My father also told me that he saw and spoke with my grandmother often. When she arrived in Prague from Australia, my grandmother told him what was going on and handed him my letter.

My stepmother was cooking, and the smell I remembered as a child. The food was great, and my stepmother was a good cook. I enjoy the Czech cuisine.

I had my own bedroom with a very comfortable bed. Each morning my father brought me coffee in bed. He knew I liked coffee, and he drank Turkish coffee. I asked him "how could you drink that thick, syrupy Turkish coffee?" He replied, "I like strong coffee". I guess that is where I get the taste for strong coffee from!

I asked my father to take me to the places that I could remember when I was nine, especially my old school and where I lived before going to Australia. He took me to the flat, I lived in. An old lady came out next door to the flat we lived in, and my father and she spoke in Czech. She said she remembered me, that I was the white-haired little girl who ran around. We went to other places I could remember and describe. I think my father was tired, but he did not complain.

My father also took me to a castle with a lake nearby. The castle had a bear enclosure. I felt sorry for the bears because the enclosure was small, and there were two bears. The castle was built in the fourteenth century, but it was kept in order and displayed how the people lived in that era. Although the Russians stole rare tapestries, paintings, and gold from the castle, the Czech people commenced restoration of the castle.

We had lunch at the outside restaurant. It was a warm day, so we drank beer. I don't normally like beer, but the Czech beer is from Pilzen and very nice.

My father also took me to meet his friends and colleagues. From what I could pick up from the language of his friends and colleagues, he was very respected and loved. His friends said, roughly translated, "How does an ugly old man like you have such a beautiful daughter?" My father was also extremely intelligent and had training as a professional, but he could not practice his profession, because of the Russian invasion.

He also spoiled me by buying me beautiful Bohemian crystal, some very rare and large pieces. I have them to this day. He also bought me a red bell. When I ring it, it reminds me of him.

One weekend Dad and my stepmother travelled to Bratislava, Slovakia for an event, and my half-sister and I had the unit to ourselves. We bought sparkling red wine, which is like champagne only a lot better. We drank quite a bit of it and were drunk. We were rolling around on the floor laughing when Dad and my stepmother walked in. Dad was not angry. In fact, he laughed at us being drunk. I know the next day we had sore heads.

On another outing, we went to a tavern in the countryside. Dad ordered two beers and asked the barman to put a green liquor into the beer. The liquor, being oily, formed an eye floating on top of the beer. I have never seen anything like it. The Czech Republic is known for its beer, and some of the liquors are very strong and have high alcohol content.

It was summer, and Dad took us to the chalet (weekend house) they had in the forest, not far from Prague. The chalet was built on a cliff, and you could see and hear the fast-moving river below. From where I slept, I could see the forest. Every night, a beautiful snowy owl sat in the tree, outside my window, hooted and watched me. It was so peaceful.

There were no hot showers and no running water. To have a bath, you had to go outside. There was no privacy around the bathtub, and I asked Dad what happened if someone walked by. He replied, "You better hurry up". The water was freezing, so I washed as quickly as I could and got out. Dad thought it was funny. I was shivering.

Because of Dad's knowledge from his time as a ranger, he took us out into the forest to pick mushrooms. You need to be very careful and know which ones are not poisonous. People have picked poisonous mushrooms and gotten very sick and rushed to the hospital.

I was out with my half-sister and her boyfriend, and when we got home, Dad told me to come outside on the balcony because he had a surprise for me. A dead deer was hanging on the balcony. I asked Dad, "What are you going to do with it?" He told me he would eat it. I was shocked. I said, "You killed Bambi". Dad laughed and explained that when animals got old or sick, the most humane thing is to kill them. My stepmother cooked the deer. It was delicious but very rich.

Between travelling from London to Prague. Bruce and I invited my half-sister to come to London and have a holiday. She agreed and was so excited because she had not travelled anywhere until then. We paid for her air ticket. It was summer in England, so Bruce and I decided to take her on a holiday around England. We went to a lot of places. My half-sister loved chocolate mint biscuits and mint and chocolate ice-cream, and she could not get enough of it. We took her to a seaside village in Cornwall, England, where we bought fish and chips, she absolutely loved it. The only fish available in the Czech Republic, is carp, a mud oily tasting fish. Carp is served for Christmas dinner with a potato salad, in the Czech Republic. I like fish, but carp is disgusting, something I don't miss.

It was also a time when the IRA was active in London and elsewhere in England. My half-sister and I caught a train from London to a place outside of London where we lived. This place had a very large army presence and camp, so it was a perfect target for the IRA.

The train was approximately two kilometres from this place when it stopped. We were told the IRA had left a bomb on the railway tracks at the train station, and buses were organized to take us to where we lived. I could see the fear on my half-sister's face (and realized she probably thought of the communist rule), but I reassured her that everything would be okay.

CHAPTER 13

Back and Forth to London and Prague. Tragedy - My Father's Death.

From January 1990 to approximately February 1991, my father organized a visa where I could enter the Czech Republic as often and whenever I liked. I travelled from London to Prague every month and stayed for approximately a fortnight to spend time with my father and my new family.

As I said, it was the best time in my life, not only to finally find and meet my father but to discover my new family, who were not dysfunctional and showed love towards me. I felt loved and safe, and I could be myself.

My father invited Bruce and me to spend Christmas in 1990, in Prague. I was unsure of taking Bruce. Nevertheless, we travelled to Prague. Bruce complained and whined about everything. I ignored him and had a great time. After that, I never invited Bruce anywhere as our marriage was not doing well, and it was obvious he was not comfortable in Prague. I travelled to Prague in early January 1991. I did not expect what

I saw and heard. My father had become very ill and was put into palliative care. He was dying; the doctors said they could not do anything for him except keep him comfortable and lessen the pain.

He was dying of cancer and had a pneumonia complication. Doctors could not believe that with cancer, Dad was still cross-country skiing. He could come home on weekends when he was up to it. He became very thin and gaunt. The last time I saw my father was a weekend he came home.

I prayed and prayed that he would get well.

I was working in the corporate legal department of a large firm outside London in 1991. I was in a meeting with my boss and some of my colleagues when a girl came in and handed me a handwritten message, telling me my father died. I remember everything going black, and it was very hot. I was told I collapsed on the floor, screaming and screaming, and then I became unconscious. I was rushed to the hospital and diagnosed with an emotional breakdown, panic attack, and severe depression.

When I was released from the hospital with medication and sedatives, my family doctor came to my home and told me I had a miscarriage. When he told me, I had no reaction. I lay in bed well over a week, not wanting to move.

I improved very slightly but could not go back to work. I was referred to a psychiatrist and a grief counselor, but nothing helped. I felt that my world was turned upside down, and there were darkness and pain. I could not stop crying even though on medication.

My half-sister's boyfriend contacted me and told me I needed to come to Prague for the reading of dad's will. I arrived in Prague depressed and angry because I was not allowed to say goodbye to my father and was not invited to the funeral. When my father became ill, my stepmother, I believe out of shock and grief, was not nice to me. But I understand how she felt.

At the solicitor's office, there was me, my half-sister and her boyfriend. I cannot remember whether my stepmother was there. The will was read out in Czech. I had trouble understanding the language, so my half-sister's boyfriend translated it for me. He basically said Dad left me something, but it was of no significance. I do recall Dad telling me he left me some land in Prague. The way I felt, depressed and grief-stricken, I thought, *I have just arrived on the scene, and Dad passed away. My half-sister was with him most of his life.* I did not know what I wanted to do, so I let my inheritance to go to her. Today, I wish one day, I could have a home in Prague and live there permanently. It is also my wish, and since my mother did not tell me about my father's side of the family or that of her own, about her sisters or cousins. I pray that one day, I am able to find an aunt or cousin, not only to get to know them but also find out about my childhood, which to this day there are still pieces missing in the jigsaw puzzle.

My relationship with Bruce had not been good for quite some time. It had deteriorated rapidly. He was angry with me about going to Prague all the time. I think he was jealous. Because of my father's death, and the relationship failing with Bruce, all I could think of doing was to go back to Australia.

My mental health had not improved, and my relationship with Bruce was beyond repair, so I decided I would go back to Australia. In July 1992, I told Bruce I was going back to Australia on my own, and I did not want him to come with me or follow me. What I didn't know until Bruce followed me to Australia was the real reason, he married me.

I packed up all my things, including crockery and some furniture, and shipped them to Australia. I left for Australia approximately in August 1992. Bruce eventually followed me, and that was when I found out the only reason, he married me was to stay in Australia permanently.

Chapter 14

Conclusion

Some people go through life without experiencing any highs or lows. My life has been anything but boring, and there were many times I was in dangerous situations. I always felt there was someone looking after me, guiding me out of these situations. Experiencing these situations is not much fun, but it has made me the person I am today.

Finding my father was the greatest joy in my life. Losing him only a year or so after finding him broke me and changed me. I still miss him, but I am very grateful that I met him and had him for a short time. It is said that "A daughter's first love is her father". This is so true, but unfortunately, I met that first love when I was about twenty-nine years old. I am grateful I had him for that short time rather than not at all. I believe we both knew we would meet each other someday and that he was sick for quite some time. Then when we finally met and spent some time together, he could let go.

I have been fortunate to travel to Prague every couple of years and see my family. And now I have a beautiful niece. When I travel to Prague, I go to his resting place. He is in an urn and behind a glass window. I sit there and talk to him.

I have been called strong. Yet at times, I want to curl up and not be so strong. But the old cliché, "What doesn't kill you makes you stronger", is true.

I also believe there is a reason for everything—positive and negative. I cannot think what the reason is for me being in dangerous situations, my mother and stepfather abusing me, and then finding my father and losing him. Perhaps in time, it will be revealed to me.

If this book can help just one person, then writing it was well worth it.